THE WAY WE WERE

THE BRITISH AT WORK

★ ★ ★

TIM GLYNNE-JONES

AURA

This edition published in 2016
by Baker & Taylor UK Ltd,
Bicester, Oxfordshire, OX26 4ST

Copyright © Arcturus Holdings Limited
26/27 Bickels Yard, 151–153 Bermondsey Street
London SE1 3HA

ISBN: 978-1-78599-671-9
AD005267UK

Printed in China

THE WAY WE WERE

THE BRITISH AT WORK

★ ★ ★

Contents

....

Introduction

As a small industrial nation, Britain was punching way above its weight as it entered the 20th century. The First World War ramped up the nation's industrial output and brought women into workplaces that were previously the sole preserve of men. After the war, the shortage of manpower and the desire to rebuild brought a period of boom followed by the bust of the Great Depression. *The British at Work* takes up that story…

It begins with a portrait of British workers between the wars – the jobs they did, the way they dressed, the places they worked – then moves on to the Second World War and the postwar years, and finally into the era of prosperity and progress, characterized by Prime Minister Harold Macmillan as a period in which 'most of our people have never had it so good'.

Judge for yourself whether or not he was right. What we see is a Britain on the move, inextricably caught up in a quest for progress that brought many new jobs – the ice cream man, the pilot, the TV presenter – but also threatened to kill off many others – the miner, the shipbuilder, the lighthouse operator.

The working day was also changing. Rarer became the sight of factory workers pouring out of the gates to walk home to their terraced houses just around the corner; in their place came the stereotypical commuter, riding the train from the suburbs into London with newspaper, furled umbrella and cigarette.

The role of women in the workplace was changing too. Invited into light industrial roles to help the war effort, women seized their chance to push for reforms that would give them equal opportunities to work in whatever field they chose. That particular change was slow in coming, though. For the most part, it was nurse, teacher or dancer for a young woman who wanted to earn her own living.

It's all here in *The British at Work*, intriguingly captured in the photographs of the time, with some additional words of explanation alongside.

Golden Years

The years between the wars were personified by contrasting moods of boundless enthusiasm and deep despair. The men who returned to work after the First World War were thankful just to be alive; within a decade they would be happy just to have a job.

The death toll of the war had had a profound effect on both the nation's psyche and its manpower. Britain bounced back with a determination not only to rebuild but also to live life to the full. In order to do so, it needed everybody, men and women alike, to roll their sleeves up and lend their weight to the cause.

Cinema, television and the motor car promised to drive society forward into a new golden age, underpinned by improvements in healthcare and education. Change was slow in coming, though, and the Great Depression slowed it further still. On the roads, motorized transport mingled with horse and cart; flower girls sold posies to stockbrokers; photographers took pictures of redundant shipyards. By the end of the 1930s, the country was on the rise again – but a very dark cloud lay ahead.

Left *No hard hats, no hi-viz, no scaffolding… just a couple of straps and a lot of pluck keeps these workers safe as they apply a bit of spit and polish to the bronze horses on top of Wellington Arch, above Hyde Park Corner in London.*

The word 'scavenger' comes from the Old English for a customs collector. By the 1920s, it had assumed a very different meaning. This 'scavenger boy' keeps body and soul together by clearing up droppings left in the street behind the horse-drawn vehicles of London.

'She's been smiling all day up until now.' A family portrait photographer waits for the optimum moment during a domestic shoot in 1935. It was the year Kodachrome colour film was introduced, but black and white was still the norm, and would remain so for another 30 years.

ANIMALS FREE
TREATED

FLOOD VICTIMS
COLLECTED

Contributions

1920 saw an amendment to the Veterinary Surgeons Act to provide vets with a regular income for the first time. The demand for veterinary skills is evident in this queue of dog-owners waiting to have their pets treated by a mobile vet, working out of a horse-drawn wagon.

A far cry from the modern automated car production line, a team of 10 men work on the assembly of a 1930 Bentley racing car in Welwyn, with an 11th overseeing for quality control. The British automotive industry was approaching its heyday, with no fewer than 25 different manufacturers in operation.

'Do you have vertigo?'
'Only as far as the bus stop!'
A gang of construction workers show no fear as they perch on the steel
frame of a building in London during their lunch break, while down below
a steady flow of omnibuses enjoys the absence of heavy traffic.

Chips with everything

....

The growth in motorized transport in the 1930s brought other luxuries, such as the mobile fast food van – a concept that would last to the present day. In those days, fast food meant fish and chips; the burger, pizza and kebab were unheard of and Friday night's treat would be the British classic of cod or haddock, coated in batter and deep-fried in boiling hot beef dripping, then served with a steaming portion of chips, liberally sprinkled with salt and vinegar.

The mobile fish and chip van became a common sight in the 1930s and the way they were fitted out became more sophisticated to make the most of demand. The dripping was heated in coal-fired fryers and vans would drive around several locations in one evening – hot and hard work for the men on board, who could dish out 100 portions an hour when business was brisk.

The men working this fish and chip van have been descended upon by a group of young lads in Morden, south London.

'Keep your germs, please.' Two saleswomen at a café in London take precautions against the influenza epidemic gripping the capital. Even in the 1930s, memories were still fresh from the deadly 1918 flu pandemic estimated to have killed as many as 100 million people worldwide; no one was taking any chances.

While they were barred from many careers, one job women were allowed to do was firefighting. Girls' fire brigades were often formed in schools and colleges, but also operated as private entities before the formation of the National Fire Service. Interestingly, it would take until 1982 before the appointment of the first woman professional public firefighter.

Teaching was another popular career for women before the war. Greater access to education since the turn of the century had given them the qualifications to pass on their knowledge and skills to the next generation. This teacher is rehearsing Christmas carols with a group of orphaned children at a Barnardo's home in Barkingside, Essex.

Certain events could always bring work to a halt, such as a king's speech or a major sporting occasion. These workers, labouring on a Saturday afternoon in 1931, have taken a break to listen to the BBC's live radio broadcast of the Grand National from Aintree.

'If you want to get ahead, get a hat.' Before the bowler hat became the ubiquitous headgear for workers in the City of London, the trilby was the common accessory for workers in the nation's financial centre, or, for certain establishments, the more intimidating top hat.

Right *The role of men and women in society is shown emphatically in this scene of a Welsh miner being washed by his wife after a gruelling shift down the pit. With black coal dust smothering his cheeks and hair, he yields to her cleansing touch before dinner, bed and then doing it all again the next day.*

Shipbuilders in Glasgow's Clydebank shipyard are dwarfed by the massive hull of the Queen Mary. Work on the ship was halted for several years due to the Great Depression, leaving many of Glasgow's shipyard workers in dire straits. The merger of the Cunard and White Star lines saw an upturn and the ship was launched in 1936.

Between the wars, many jobs became available for women in light industry as factories became more automated. In a scene reminiscent of Chicken Run, *these women are polishing razor blades at the Gillette factory in Brentford, while their male foreman watches on in a classically domineering pose.*

In an altogether more relaxed, spacious setting that looks like it could almost be part of the Members' Stand at Lords, four workers in Tonbridge, Kent, spend their day making cricket balls. This skilled craft involved winding twine around a cork core and then stitching it into a leather outer cover.

Factory workers at de Havilland's aircraft factory in Hatfield, Hertfordshire, celebrate being given a special day off. You could call it a performance-related bonus, coming as it did as a reward for building the DH88 Comet that famously won the MacRobertson Air Race from England to Australia in 1934.

Following the Great Depression that spread from the USA in 1929, Britain's economy began to pick up from 1934 onwards. In this picture from that year, traders from the London Stock Exchange gather outside to discuss the upturn in fortunes as they wait for the markets to open.

The popularity of chorus lines and modern dance revues, as well as a rising interest in ballet, spearheaded by Ballet Rambert and the Vic-Wells Ballet during the 1930s, saw many young women pursue a career in dancing. The money wasn't great, but it offered a rare taste of creative freedom.

In a scene from 1933 reminiscent of My Fair Lady, *two flower girls peddle roses and hydrangeas from a pitch in London's Piccadilly Circus. Not so young and pretty as Eliza Doolittle perhaps, but the chirpy Cockney character is evident in their grinning faces.*

The clock is ticking for this steeplejack working on
the giant clock on the Shell Mex building in London's
Strand, as he strives to get his measuring done before
quarter past three! The clock is 50 metres off the
ground and he's wearing a trilby hat.

As George Orwell said, 'Our civilization is founded on coal.' In addition to firing the factories and machines, coal was the fuel that kept most people's home fires burning, so coal hawkers like this woman in Winsford, Cheshire were a vital cog in the whole operation of 1930s living.

Right *While the men knock the walls down, the women make the tea. More sexual role-play in evidence as hospital maids from Moorfields Eye Hospital in London distribute cups of tea with saucers to keep the demolition crew refreshed. But women were beginning to break down metaphorical walls too.*

Railways workers on a signal gantry above the LNER mainline in Hatfield, Hertfordshire, maintain the signals that keep the Flying Scotsman *on track. With trains hurtling past at speeds well in excess of 100mph, the signalman's job carried enormous responsibility, as well as the physical demands of pulling the levers that operated the signals mechanically.*

*To the shock and outrage of some men, and indeed women, female
participation in occupations previously regarded as bastions of
masculinity included an encroachment into sports commonly regarded
as 'male'. Women's wrestling originated in the Lancashire and
Yorkshire mills and by the 1930s it was gaining a hold in London.*

Chelsea footballers in training display their aerial prowess. The job of a professional footballer was a predominantly working-class occupation and foreign labour was almost unheard of, with teams throughout the Football League being made up of English, Scottish, Welsh and Irish players.

One field that was largely supplied by foreign labour was the circus. The woman being nibbled by the elephant is none other than Maria Rasputin, daughter of the notorious Russian monk. Renowned as a fearless animal trainer, she found employment in the 1930s, wowing the circus crowds of Britain.

Right *The mournful cry of the rag and bone man – by the 1960s, a dying breed immortalized in the sitcom* Steptoe and Son *– would have children running into the street as he plodded his horse and cart around the neighbourhood collecting 'any old iron' that people wanted to throw out.*

The image of Father Christmas was fairly well established by the 1930s and the job of playing Santa at the local department store was becoming an established tradition. It was thirsty work, though, and a major challenge for all Santas was to drink your tea without your beard coming unstuck in front of all those wide-eyed children.

Workers at Rowntree's chocolate factory in York line up to 'punch in' at the start of their shift. The time clock/punch card system was a common sight in factories, providing a printed record of when a worker arrived for work and when they left. In the 1930s, the number of hours you were expected to work fell on average from 64 to 58 per week.

With labour cheap, employers could afford to throw manpower at jobs that might be done by one or two people today. This team of decorators are making short work of painting the new Empire Pool at Wembley in preparation for the Empire Games in 1934.

All aboard the smoking carriage

Suit, tie, newspaper, cigarette – the standard uniform of the British businessman on his commute to work. The concept of commuting had evolved in the 19th century when the rise of the railways had led to a growing distance between home and the workplace. However, even in the 1930s the majority of Britons walked to work, with the daily use of public transport being mostly restricted to those people working in the larger cities.

Despite the steep rise in private car ownership, most commuters continued to use public transport rather than drive. It was not an experience people cherished, though. The railways were privately run for profit and there were always grumbles over ticket prices and conditions, especially on London Underground. Crowded trains and smoke from the engine mingling with smoke from cigarettes and pipes created an environment one commentator described as 'a form of mild torture which no person would undergo if he could conveniently help it'.

Pushing wooden sleds, known as mud horses, designed to skate across the mud flats rather than sink into them, two fishermen at Stolford in Somerset return from the water's edge. They have been setting nets to catch mainly shrimp, but any fish, such as cod, sea bass, dog fish or eel, would come as a welcome bonus.

Two young women at Bevingtons leather factory in Bermondsey, London, work together 'liming' hides. This was a smelly, unpleasant process that involved dipping the animal skins in a mixture of lime and water to remove traces of flesh and hair. The rawhides were then taken to be washed before tanning.

On the map

....

Ever wondered how maps are made? Two cartographers get on top of their work drawing a detailed map at the Ordnance Survey office in Southampton. Working from land survey data and perhaps some aerial photography, the draughtsmen were employed to draw the maps by hand.

1935 saw the launch of the Retriangulation of Great Britain, a campaign to bring the charted record of the whole nation up to date. This gargantuan task involved sending out surveyors to erect triangulation pillars (Trig Points) atop wind- and rain-blasted peaks throughout the land. The surveyors had to work in all conditions, being soaked, frozen and battered by driving winds as they lugged their rocks and stones to bleak, remote hilltops. If they were lucky they would have a horse to help.

By 1962 the task was complete. Around 6,500 Trig Points were built in all and such a good job did the surveyors do that they remain firmly in place to this day.

Air crew unload Russian gold from a plane at Croydon Airport. Croydon was London's major airport before the Second World War and the call for air crew was growing fast, although most air transport was still for freight rather than passenger purposes.

A father with his sons, each one following in the family business. Though theirs was grimy and sometimes dangerous work, sweeps enjoyed a sense of freedom in their lofty workplace on the rooftops. They used to call 'hee-hee-hee' down the chimney to make sure they had the right house.

Children had to work too – of course they did! School was compulsory up to the age of 14 and you sat in rows at wooden desks while the teacher scribbled your lessons in chalk on a blackboard. There was no uniform and most children walked to and from school.

*Cattle breeders, three of whom look like they might have sprung
from the same bull, take a well-earned rest as they wait for the
opening of the 1935 Royal Agricultural Show. The show was a
100-year-old tradition for the farming community and provided
breeders with the chance to show off their year's work.*

With the most mechanized war in history just around the corner, the use of wooden horses to teach new recruits how to ride seems quaintly futile. But the art of horsemanship was a cornerstone of the British military and these training dummies at Aldershot enabled trainees to learn the basics before mounting the real thing.

Left *A page boy from Glasgow with a doorman outside the Trocadero in London's Piccadilly. Glasgow was particularly hard hit during the Great Depression, forcing many people to travel in search of work. This lad has found employment running messages and deliveries between London hotels.*

Above *At the Great Western Railway works in Hayes, Middlesex, two men load special cylinders with sleepers to be impregnated with creosote. In this efficient manufacturing process, up to 600 sleepers at a time were rolled into the cylinders on wagons, the doors sealed shut and the creosote applied.*

When the lack of work bit hard, coal and shipyard workers from Jarrow in County Durham marched to London to petition Parliament in 1936. The Jarrow Marchers were provided with food and drink by supporters along the route of their 280-mile walk and supporters like Labour MP Ellen Wilkinson (centre) joined the march.

'So who's for shearing first?' Two farmers from Sussex, sporting beards that even modern Shoreditch would marvel at, admire their woolly charges in a pen at Findon Sheep Fair. Dating back to 1261, the fair was a chance to share new ideas in the increasingly mechanized world of livestock farming.

Not one of the more common occupations but a popular one nonetheless, the lion tamer was the star turn of many a circus or travelling menagerie. The chance to see exotic beasts in the flesh was snapped up by eager audiences, who marvelled at the courage and control of those who braved the big cats.

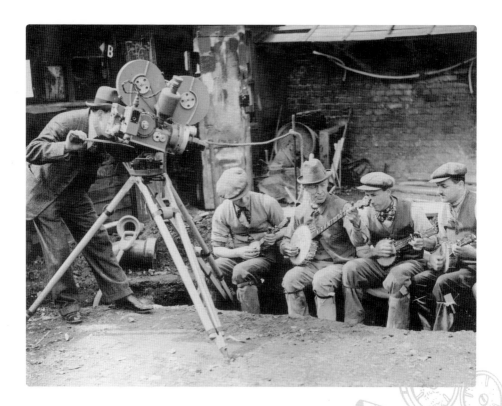

The 1930s saw the birth of a brand new occupation: the television cameraman. While the technology and techniques had already been developed in cinematography, the subject matter tended to be more everyday, such as these labourers from Lewisham, London, making music together in their lunch break in 1936.

Three king penguins do the rounds of their enclosure at London Zoo in 1936, inspecting the work of a gang of decorators and secretly hoping one of them will ping off their platform into the pool. With no faster way of applying the paint than by brush, large decorating jobs like this were a case of 'many hands make light work'.

Two nurses from the British Red Cross tend to the wounded head of a young hop-picker in Kent. Nursing was a popular occupation for women who wanted to work and there were plenty of casualties for them to tend to, like these hop-pickers from the East End of London.

Left *Not so much bringing the house down as helping to put it up, the famous Lancashire comedienne and singer Gracie Fields serenades builders working on the reconstruction of the Prince of Wales Theatre in London's West End in 1937, having laid the foundation stone for the new building.*

Above *All smiles at the end of the day's work. Employees from the KLG spark plug factory in Putney, most of them young women, set out on their journey home. The factory workforce generally lived within walking distance and those with bicycles could be home in minutes.*

The mundanity of the conveyor belt is etched on the faces of these factory workers, packing Court Biscuits at the Caley biscuit factory in Norwich, 1937. The production line provided a chance to chat with the people around you, but if you didn't get on it could be a very long day.

Lost in earnest conversation, hat-wearing cotton traders mingle on the floor of the Royal Exchange in Manchester. The original Cottonopolis, Manchester was the centre of Britain's cotton industry and trading continued at the Royal Exchange until 1968, but the interwar years saw a dramatic decline, with the loss of nearly 350,000 jobs.

'And smile!' The photographer does a commendable job of cajoling a whole factory floor into pausing their needlework to smile for the camera at the same time. The noise of a factory full of sewing machines could be quite deafening, which could be why these women look so grateful for a moment's break from work.

'So, how are you on the offside law?' A trainee football referee
from Essex, already mastering the requisite hangdog expression,
is tested on his knowledge of the Laws of the Game. Refereeing
was not a full-time job, but one carried out usually by policemen or
ex-Army officers who were comfortable with authority.

In a reversal of the classic wartime scenario, recruits from the 3rd Women's Territorial Service kiss the men in their life goodbye as they prepare to board a train bound for training camp. With trouble brewing in Germany, the Armed Forces became an increasingly fruitful source of work for women in the late-1930s.

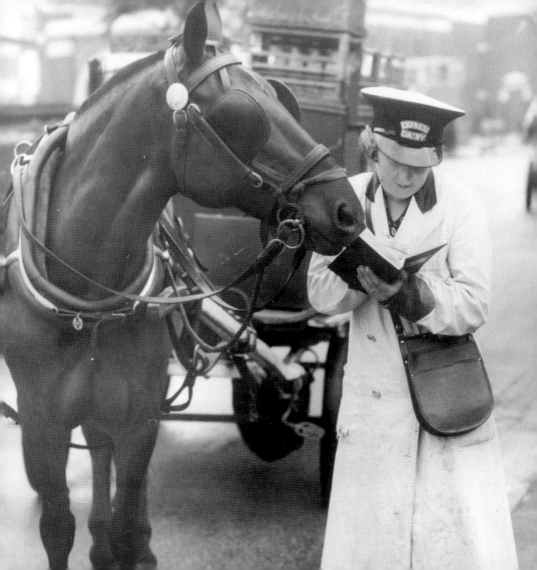

Wartime and Beyond

The Second World War breathed new life into Britain's heavy industries like shipbuilding and coal mining, and the munitions factories roared into life once again. 'Manning' the lathes and welding torches was an army of women, stepping up to keep the country working while the men were away at the war. Women worked in the factories, women dug the fields, women delivered the milk, waited the tables and kept home – and a generation of empowered women emerged.

The postwar years saw an emphasis on technological advancement. Britain had entered the atomic age. Jet engines and computers signposted the future, not the austere, heavy industries upon which the empire had been built. Social attitudes were becoming less weighed down by history too. Entertainment grew more risqué, theatre more thought-provoking… the old Victorian attitudes had died during the war and Britons began to raise their working ambitions beyond the walls of the factory at the end of the road. They could travel now, seek work in a new town, learn new skills and make money.

Left *Before the Second World War, milkmen were exactly that: men. During the war women stepped in to make sure the nation received its daily delivery, with the help of the faithful horse and cart. Not many horses were capable of checking the entries in the order book, though.*

Left *For the Armed Forces, new weaponry and machines meant learning new skills. In this exercise, a Naval seaman peers through the porthole at the bottom of a 15 foot tank to receive signals from his instructor as he trains for service aboard a submarine.*

Right *Even in wartime, certain standards had to be maintained, and that included pride in the nation's appearance. Here, two steeplejacks mount a somewhat flimsy-looking scaffold to polish the copper globe and galleon on top of the Cook's building in Ludgate Circus, London.*

The nippy

One of the most recognizable brand icons of the first
half of the century was the Lyons Corner House waitress,
or 'nippy', as they were known, because of the speed
at which they nipped from table to table. Their uniform
comprised a short black dress with 30 pairs of purely
decorative white pearl buttons, stitched on with red thread,
a white collar and white detachable cuffs, a white square
apron, dark stockings, black shoes and a white maid's cap
with a black band incorporating the Lyons badge. Dolls
could be bought dressed in the familiar Lyons uniform.

Nippies were expected to look after their own uniform,
which meant paying for laundering out of their weekly
wage of 26 shillings, for which they had to put in 54
hours' work! If they worked weekends, they could earn
an extra two shillings and sixpence. It was tiring work,
always on their feet attending to an endless stream of
customers in the popular tea houses.

The two contrasting sides of Covent Garden are captured in one frame in 1939. A fruit and veg trader from the famous market stands in front of his stall as a finely dressed couple on their way to the Opera House cut a dash across the flagstones.

*It looks like a riot breaking out or perhaps people fleeing from a madman,
but the catalyst that's sparked this particular scene is nothing more than a
change in interest rates at the Bank of England in 1939. The men running are
messengers heading off to carry the news back to their workplaces.*

Charwomen (or charladies if you were being genteel) enjoying a cup of char (tea). Forerunners of the modern 'cleaner', charwomen were domestic cleaners who generally did the rounds of several employers. The pinafore, or 'pinnie', was the standard apparel, often accessorised with a head scarf.

Wall's ice cream girls

Another job that became the preserve of women during the Second World War was ice cream vendor. Wall's had the biggest ice cream factory in the world, in Gloucester, and their ice cream trikes took to the streets from more than 100 depots around the country. When the men went off to war, the girls stepped up to keep the ice cream moving.

While mobile fish and chip vans were becoming quite commonplace, the motorized ice cream van was yet to appear on Britain's streets. Instead, the goods were wheeled around in cold boxes mounted on the front of tricycles, bearing the famous slogan 'Stop me and buy one'. If someone stopped you halfway up a hill, it came as welcome relief from some strenuous pedalling.

The ice creams they sold were good and basic: 'bricks' of vanilla ice cream were most in demand from households that had yet to discover the benefits of the domestic freezer.

Left *The Second World War gave women the opportunity to prove that they were just as capable as men when it came to a wide variety of industrial jobs. This lathe operator is making a valuable contribution to the war effort, manufacturing weapons in an armaments factory.*

Above *While more and more women were going out to work, the job of keeping home also demanded full-time attention and nobody blanched at the term 'housewife'. These Glasgow housewives have no hot water at home, let alone washing machines, so they have come to the municipal wash house, or 'steamie', to do the laundry.*

Land girls became symbols of Britain's war effort and the spirit of 'mucking in'. With large areas of land reclaimed for growing food, the land girls were a vital source of agricultural labour. These land girls are bringing in the wheat from a reclaimed field in Sussex.

With national security high on the agenda, the police played a key role in carrying out spot checks on people's identity papers, like these officers stopping traffic on a road into London. They were also having to adapt to the increase in motorized transport on Britain's roads.

'It's not all sitting around and stroking baby tigers, you know.' These
keepers at Whipsnade Zoo enjoy some quality time with three of the zoo's
recent additions, but their workload increased on the outbreak of war as a
number of animals had to be evacuated to Whipsnade from London Zoo.

A handful of ha'pennies

In 1940 the price for riding on a London bus rose by a staggering 50 per cent... from one penny to one-and-a-half pennies. These cheerful-looking bus conductors display all the ha'pennies they've been left with after their first day of collecting the new fares.

Bus conductors had a very responsible job. They were effectively the captain of the bus, responsible for its safety and for making sure every passenger paid their fare. It meant that the buses spent very little time at the stops, just long enough for passengers to get on and off. The conductor would then come round and collect their fares while the bus was on the move.

They wore uniforms with peaked caps and kept the money in a large leather pouch worn on a strap round the neck. They invariably had remarkable powers of recall, noting who got on where, who still needed to pay and who wanted to get off when.

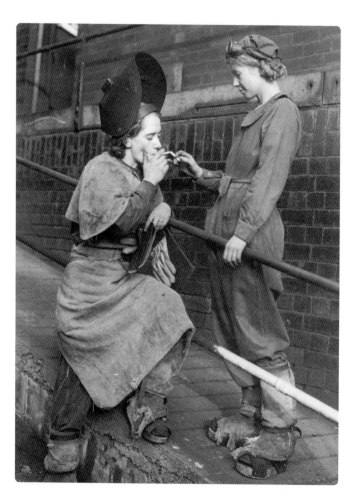

Two women welders in 1942, sporting goggles, face mask, hood, leather apron and gloves, take a break from the heat of the factory floor to share a smoke outside. Women like these worked hard in gruelling conditions to keep the steel mills operating throughout the Second World War.

Women work on the production line at the Austin car plant in Birmingham, applying the final touches in 1945. Behind the row of gleaming new Austin Sixteens is a line of Austin K2 army ambulances, signalling the transition from wartime transport to the bright new era of postwar motoring.

Windmill Girls adopt one of their more demure poses for the BBC camera. In normal circumstances the Windmill Girls pushed the boundaries of public acceptability with their dance shows and nude appearances at the notorious Windmill Theatre in London's Soho.

The never-say-die wartime spirit prevailed in the postwar years as Britain's workers faced the next battle of getting the country back on its feet. This milkman from Cheam, Surrey, isn't going to let a little bit of snow stop him making his rounds – though it might take a little longer than normal.

Right In the years immediately after the war there was a shortage of manpower in Britain, so having more than one string to your bow was an advantage. Fred Digby (standing) is a cowman from Essex who doubles as a barber, providing haircuts for his colleagues on the farm.

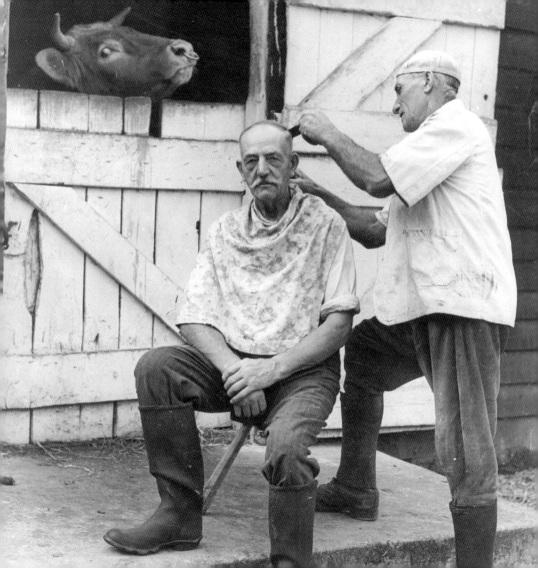

As Britain's leaders tried to rebuild the country, they provided ammunition for newspaper cartoonists. This shows some of the nation's finest, including Giles of the Express *(left) and Norman Pett, creator of* Jane *for the* Daily Mirror *(front right) with Illingworth of the* Daily Mail *just behind, at a life drawing class in the White Swan pub just off Fleet Street.*

Tea break brings a shoal of Yarmouth herring curers crowding into the works canteen for their dose of the revitalizing brew. The tradition of the tea break dated back to the early 19th century and, despite some attempts to abolish it, survived as a mainstay of the working day.

A dog's life

• •

A man clutches a litter of puppies at Club Row pet market in the East End of London. Club Row was one of the more unusual work places in Britain, furnishing the money-making ambitions of a bizarre menagerie of dodgy salesmen with vanloads of puppies. The market took place on a Sunday, just off Bethnal Green Road, and in the early days it specialized in exotic birds. By the 1960s, however, it had evolved into a market place for just about every species of animal you could imagine – from fish and frogs to snakes, monkeys and even lion cubs.

Where these animals came from was anyone's guess. Where they were going to was more of a bone of contention. Anything fluffy would attract the attention of visiting children, who would beg their parents to buy the thing, regardless of what it actually was and how well suited it might be to the average British household. Club Row became the focus for animal rights campaigners, who would turn up every week to protest at the treatment of the creatures on sale there. There were claims that cats and dogs were being offloaded wholesale for vivisection and the market was eventually closed down in 1983.

Haymakers take a break for lunch on a farm in Hampshire. With horse-drawn machinery still the state of the art in farm machinery, haymaking in the postwar years remained a communal activity requiring as many hands as possible to bring in the crop before the weather turned.

In the more permissive postwar years, there arose a demand for glamour and nightclub entertainment, with chorus girls fuelling a fantasy world in the centre of London. It was hard work for the girls, who danced and sang their way around the fleshpots of Soho, putting on several performances a night.

Right *It wasn't just the girls. Men were becoming inclined to drop their trousers too, given half a chance. This is one of the Rudell Trio, a troupe of trampolinists, rehearsing for a performance that involves a cheeky striptease at the London Palladium in 1949.*

Left *Ex-timpanist with the Symphony Orchestra of Venezuela, Trinidadian Edmundo Ros moved to London in 1937 and became a household name. He re-recorded Broadway hits to a Latin beat – mambo, cha cha cha, rumba, samba, bolero, meringe, whatever. In 1949, he sold three million copies of 'The Wedding Samba' in 78 format, and no one else could carry off rumba sleeves the way he did.*

Right *Jack Hylton was a prominent band leader between the wars but became a highly successful theatre impresario in the postwar era with productions such as* Kiss Me Kate *and* The Merry Widow *to his name. In this photo he watches from the wings as one of his productions takes shape.*

The Road to Prosperity

In 1957, Prime Minister Harold Macmillan made a speech to a Conservative party rally in Bedford. He roused the crowd with a picture of unprecedented prosperity. 'Let us be frank about it,' he told his audience, 'most of our people have never had it so good.'

And so the era was encapsulated in one phrase. In many ways Macmillan was right. An increase in production in industry and agriculture had led to increased wages, more consumer spending and a higher standard of living. The country's fortunes appeared to be in a virtuous circle of supply and demand, with plenty of modern conveniences to spend your wages on. Macmillan, though, warned against getting carried away.

He was right too. It soon proved that the peaking fortunes of the heavy industries were, in fact, their death throes. Britain's shipbuilding, coal mining and motor industries' days were numbered. Manpower was being replaced by machine power. But new industries were emerging, with greater emphasis on the value of entertainments like sport, television and art. It was time for Britain's workforce to think again.

Left *A lorry load of families from one of London's poorer neighbourhoods arrives in Kent for the start of the hop-picking season. This annual opportunity for work brought thousands of Londoners, including women and children, out to the Garden of England for four weeks of work and revelry at the end of summer.*

Left *It's a dirty job but someone's got to do it… Inspectors shine a light on the architectural wonder of London's sewers, which were built back in the 19th century and still going strong a century later. The sewage system was expanding with the capital and was regularly maintained to keep the capital moving freely.*

Right *Looking like something out of an episode of* Doctor Who, *this sewage worker is wearing an early form of breathing apparatus, which enables him to carry out his work clearing silt from the sewers without being overcome by fumes. Sewage workers like this were known as 'flushers'.*

Laughing all the way

The London docks were a good source of work in the 1950s and you could earn around the equivalent of £600 a week (£30 at the time). Following the Second World War there were concerns over finding sufficient manpower to keep the docks running at full capacity so there was always work to be found. The labour turned up and the docks thrived. A decade later, however, innovations such as container shipping had brought about a severe decline in fortunes for London's docks and its dockers, large numbers of whom lost their jobs.

Chief among the casualties were the lightermen: highly skilled boatmen who paddled flat-bottomed boats or 'lighters' around the Port of London, mastering the tides and currents of the river to transfer goods from ships anchored midstream to quays and warehouses along the river. The work required muscle power and an intimate knowledge of the river.

Everybody's favourite get-rich-quick scheme in the 1950s was the football pools. The potential of a life-changing payout had millions of people playing every week. This photograph of women checking coupons for one of the big Pools companies in Liverpool gives an idea of the scale of the industry.

Left *Beret – check. Cigarette – check. String of onions – check. A female onion 'Johnnie' from Brittany peddles her wares door-to-door on Britain's streets. Breton farmers had found an enthusiastic market for their onions in Britain in the 19th century and were still a familiar sight in the 1950s. They were called 'Johnnies' because so many of them had the Breton first name Yann.*

Right *A classic image of working-class Britain in the 1950s: two fishergirls in aprons and headscarves walk home through a slum area of Hull that is effectively an annex of the local fishery. The distinction between home and work was blurred, with whole communities serving the same employer.*

Left *Dance was still the glamorous career opportunity for young women in the 1950s, with prima ballerinas like Dame Margot Fonteyn providing the inspiration. But not everyone got to dance at the Royal Ballet. Here, a group of dancers relaxes between shows in the stairwell of Ciro's Club in London.*

Right *'By his hat shall ye know the man.' The flat crowned hat (not to mention the bloodstained apron and the indelible aroma of fish) was the distinguishing mark of the porters at Billingsgate fish market, the hub of the fish trade in London.*

TELEVISION DETECTIO

36

VAN

They're watching you

Along with the boom in television came the TV detector van, a mobile unit that could detect from the street whether a television was being used in an unlicensed house. Looking like operatives from the Cold War, this crew have detected strains of *Muffin the Mule* coming from number 62 and are preparing to pounce.

The television licence was introduced to fund the BBC in 1946, priced £2, and was administered by the General Post Office. It was not illegal to own a television without a licence; it only became an offence if you turned it on. So the detector van was introduced in 1952 to use the latest electronic gadgetry in order to check up on suspected offenders.

It was widely believed, however, that the vans were a sham – nothing more than a scare tactic by the GPO to frighten people into buying a licence. There was certainly something sinister about them.

A photographer records the beautifully coordinated scene of three steam locomotives being moved via a turntable at Ranelagh depot near Paddington in London. The age of steam was drawing to a close and the mighty engines were admired as much for their nostalgic aesthetics as for their pulling power.

A London taxi driver brushes up on his general knowledge while waiting for his next fare. Knowing what was going on in the world was important for a cabbie, but not as important as knowing the quickest route from A to B. As London expanded and its streets became more crowded, passing The Knowledge was growing harder year by year.

Actress and television announcer Avis Scott smokes a cigarette during an experiment with 3D cameras at Earls Court. Scott personified the increasingly glamorous face of television in the 1950s, but was relieved of her post as an announcer allegedly for being 'too sexy'.

Studying the form

One man who was at work while others were at play was the racecourse bookie. Only too happy to put in a decent shift in order to relieve punters of their hard-earned cash, the racecourse was the only place where it was legal to place a bet on a horse, the introduction of the licensed betting shop not taking place until 1961.

But the spirit of human enterprise prevailed and illegal bookies proliferated, mostly on the streets of working-class communities, operating their own gambling services with the threat of police raids ever present. It was largely in order to control illegal bookmaking that Harold Macmillan's government passed the Betting and Gaming Act in 1960, though it was presented as another benefit of the 'Never had it so good' age that Macmillan had proclaimed in 1957.

The on-course bookie remained a feature of a day at the races, though, preying on bumper crowds as horse racing enjoyed a boom in the postwar years.

A trainee pilot has his eyesight tested at the RAF Aircrew Selection Centre in Hornchurch, Essex. The RAF had proven its potency during the Second World War and large numbers of young men were keen to join the ranks of air heroes, now being prepared for much faster jet aircraft.

An allotment owner with his prize cabbage. During the Second World War there were an estimated 1.4 million allotments in Britain, but numbers declined after the war as prosperity increased and the growing of fresh produce became less of a necessity and more of a hobby.

The definition of temptation! A team of chocolate decorators at Rowntree's factory in York apply the finishing touches by hand to an endless procession of confectionery. Philanthropist Seebohm Rowntree played an active part in the campaign to eradicate poverty and by the 1950s his efforts had achieved almost total success.

Left *Two coal miners take a break from work. When the coal industry was nationalized in 1946, miners were the highest paid among Britain's industrial workers but their relative wages began to fall in the 1950s, with shorter working days and the increasing threat of pit closures as the coal industry went into decline.*

Above *By the 1960s the roads were rapidly filling with motorized traffic and the horse and cart were becoming a quaint anachronism. However, horse power still had its place for purveyors of stop-start delivery services, such as this coalman, doing the rounds of the Gorbals in Glasgow with his trusty steed.*

On the docks

A group of dockers from Glasgow's Clyde shipyards walks home from work, some checking their payslips, another catching up on the news. What they read was not encouraging. The world of heavy industry was changing, with precision mechanization replacing traditional skills and the demand for warships and passenger liners falling fast. The shipyards needed to modernize but many were reluctant, having witnessed the Depression that followed the rebuilding after the First World War.

While the British shipyards procrastinated, competition from abroad intensified. Eventually British yards responded with mergers and modernization and the shipyards became gargantuan wonders of towering cranes, huge, noisy machines for cutting and shaping giant steel plates, and welders hovering like fiery insects to join the parts together in a shower of sparks. The working day was arduous, but the satisfaction of seeing a ship slide down the slipway made it all worthwhile.

An ice cream man dishes out the good stuff to children on a hot summer's day. With their new motorized vans and telltale chimes, ice cream men were among the most popular workers in Britain (among children anyway), but they had to fight for their patch, literally in some cases, as competition became fierce.

Two chemists at Searle's pharmaceutical factory in High Wycombe work on the production of the new female contraceptive, known simply as 'The Pill'. They wear inflatable suits to protect them from contact with the powerful synthetic hormones, which could otherwise cause them to develop female characteristics.

Left *British boxing champion Alan Rudkin works at his day job as a porter at London's Smithfield meat market in 1970. Smithfield was known for its local pubs which would be open first thing in the morning for the night workers at the market, coming off their shift with a thirst.*

Right *Team photo of street mechanics in Notting Hill, London in 1969. Popular cars of the Sixties, the decade when motorways first became popular, included the Mini, the Ford Cortina and the Austin Cambridge. If you wanted to buy an Aston Martin DB5, it was yours for a mere £4,412.*

A lighthouse keeper sends a semaphore message to shore in 1938 from the Needles lighthouse off the coast of the Isle of Wight. Originally staffed by a crew of three – operating a 24-hour stretch, one month on/one month off – the lighthouse became fully automated in 1994.

Picture Credits
All photographs supplied by Getty Images.